DRAGONS

by John Hamilton

Published by ABDO Publishing Company, 4940 Viking Drive, Suite 622, Edina, Minnesota 55435.
Copyright ©2005 by Abdo Consulting Group, Inc. International copyrights reserved in all countries.
No part of this book may be reproduced in any form without written permission from the publisher.
ABDO & Daughters™ is a trademark and logo of ABDO Publishing Company.

Printed in the United States.

Editor: Paul Joseph
Graphic Design: John Hamilton
Cover Design: TDI
Cover Illustration: *Lord of the Skies*, ©1996 Don Maitz
Interior Photos and Illustrations: p1 *Dragons on the Sea of Night* (detail), ©1996 Don Maitz; p4 Chinese dragon, Corbis; p 5 *Lord of the Skies*, ©1996 Don Maitz; pp 6-7 *Dragons on the Sea of Night*, ©1996 Don Maitz; p 9 *Taken to Task*, ©1988 Janny Wurts; p 10 upper left: Komodo dragon, Corbis; bottom: boa constrictor, Mary Evans Picture Library; p 11 *It Takes Courage*, ©1984 Don Maitz; p 12 Marduk battling Tiamat, Mary Evans Picture Library; p 13 *Dragon Perched*, ©2004 Don Maitz; p 14 *St. George and the Dragon* by Paolo Uccello, Corbis; p 15 *Death of the Last Dragon*, ©1976 Don Maitz; p 16 oarfish, Mary Evans Picture Library; p 17 Leviathan, Mary Evans Picture Library; p 18 gargoyle, Corbis; p 19 John Lambton, Mary Evans Picture Library; p 20 *Dragon's Run*, ©1981 Janny Wurts; p 21 *Booked Flight*, ©1999 Don Maitz; pp 22-23 *Darkness at Sethanon*, ©1992 Don Maitz; p 24 wyvern, Corbis; p 25 Siegfried slays Fafnir, Corbis; p 26 Korean dragons, Corbis; p 27 *Two Dragons in Clouds* by Kano Hogai, Corbis; p 29 *Dragon's Pawn*, ©1986 Janny Wurts; p 30 *Stronghold*, ©1995 Don Maitz.

Library of Congress Cataloging-in-Publication Data

Hamilton, John, 1959–
      Dragons / John Hamilton
           p. cm. — (Fantasy & folklore)
      Includes index.
      ISBN 1-59197-711-8
      1. Dragons. I. Title.

GR830.D7H25 2004
398'.469—dc22

                                                                2004043690

CONTENTS

DRAGON TALES

"Here be dragons!"—early European mapmakers.

Dragons, of all the beasts of mythology, are the most recognized and widespread. They've appeared countless times in folklore, paintings, and movies. They populate an entire genre of fantasy literature.

Dragons represent many things to many people. These legendary monsters can be mysterious and terrifying. They are often known as firebreathing symbols of evil and chaos. But they can also be wise and heroic, bringers of rain and good fortune.

Dragons are common in many cultures worldwide. They can be found in the folk literature of England, France, Scandinavia, Greece, India, and even Central America. They are very popular in Asia, especially China and Japan. Marco Polo reported seeing dragons during his trip to China in the 13th century.

The English word dragon comes from the Greek word drakon or draca, which means serpent. Dragons come in many shapes and sizes. They are usually huge, some bigger than an elephant. Most are covered in red, gold, green, or red scales, which can be pierced by only the sharpest sword.

Left: A Chinese dragon.
Far right: Don Maitz's *Lord of the Skies*.

Dragons have long, poisonous fangs and razor-sharp talons. They have horned heads and intelligent, reptilian eyes. Western classical dragons are usually equipped with huge, batlike wings. Asian dragons also fly, but magically, without the use of wings.

Many dragons have a special gland in their throats, which allows them to exhale fire. Firebreathing is often used as a warning, but can also serve as a potent weapon of attack.

Dragons have many magical powers. Even in death, their bodies are prized by wizards and warriors. Eat the heart of a dragon, and you can magically understand the language of animals. Skin brushed with the blood of a dragon becomes impervious to swords or knives. Scatter the teeth of a dragon upon the ground, and suddenly an army of skeleton warriors is at your command.

Most dragons are content to jealously guard their treasure hoards, which are usually hidden in lairs deep underground. But when provoked, dragons beat the air with their wings and take flight, laying waste to the countryside in a firebreathing rage. Only the bravest warrior knights stand a chance against such terrifying monsters.

Left: Fantasy illustrator Don Maitz's *Dragons on the Sea of Night.*

The Origin of Dragons

re dragons real, or merely folk tales? Is it possible that a race of giant, winged lizards once existed? Many people think so, or at least think it's possible. Dragon myths can be found in many different cultures on almost every continent on Earth. It would be too much of a coincidence, many people say, for the same fictional creature to show up in so many stories.

Some people guess that dragons may be humankind's ancient memories of dinosaurs. This seems highly unlikely, though. Dinosaurs died out millions of years before people walked the earth. Even the earliest prehistoric people couldn't have a memory of a dinosaur.

Others think that dragons were a race of giant reptilian beasts that lived after the dinosaurs, dying out just as human civilization began to spread. Most scholars are skeptical of this theory also. Ancient humans painted a great many now-extinct animals on the walls of caves. You can still see these paintings today in places like France and Italy. The images include wooly mammoths, wooly rhinoceroses, bison, lions—but no dragons, or even anything resembling a giant serpent.

Far right: Taken to Task, by fantasy artist Janny Wurts.

Above: A Komodo dragon.

Some of the earliest dragon tales can be traced to the Middle East and surrounding areas, which are known for large serpents. Some explorers think a giant reptile, perhaps a surviving dinosaur, still exists in the wild, just waiting to be discovered. After all, the mountain gorillas of East Africa were unknown to science until 1902. And in 1912, a Dutch army officer brought news of a 10-foot (3-m) long "dragon" on the island of Komodo, in Indonesia. Of course, these aren't real dragons—they're monitor lizards. Still, they're the largest lizards on the planet, and the name stuck. Today they're known as Komodo dragons.

With such discoveries in mind, several dragon-hunting expeditions have focused on the deep, almost impenetrable jungles of the Republic of Congo, in central Africa, as well as the mysterious forests of Papua New Guinea. So far, the explorers have returned empty-handed.

Perhaps crocodiles, alligators, gigantic snakes, or even whales helped start the myth of dragons. Even today, huge reptiles strike terror into the hearts of many people. In December 2003, villagers in Indonesia were reported to have captured a python that measured 49 feet long (15 m) and weighed 985 pounds (447 kg). Laid out end to end, the snake would be about one and a half times as long as a city bus! Imagine a person from an earlier time encountering such a beast, then running excitedly back to his village to tell of his narrow escape from the "dragon."

Right: A 19th-century illustration of a giant boa constrictor attacking a group of boatmen in India. *Far right: It Takes Courage,* by Don Maitz.

Early Dragon Folklore

Evidence has not yet been found of real dragons. Perhaps they exist only in our imaginations. Real or not, most scholars believe that the dragons we know today come from folklore. People love to tell stories, and they especially like to create monsters that heroes can conquer. Dragons spark our imagination. They represent chaos, which is the disorder that ruled the world before civilization. Folk tales about dragons show us an evil that must be vanquished. The dragon must be defeated in order for civilization to spread.

Some scholars trace the dragon myth to ancient Babylon, 4,000 years ago. A Babylonian creation myth explains how the earth began. In the tale, Tiamat was a giant sea dragon, representing the saltwater ocean and the forces of chaos. Tiamat was eventually slain by the young god Marduk. The dragon's body was chopped in two, creating the sky and the earth. From the dragon's blood Marduk created the first humans.

As civilization spread, so too did tales of dragons. But how did the dragon myths expand outside the Middle East? How did far-flung areas like the British Isles develop

Below: Marduk, the Babylonian sun god, battles the monster Tiamat.

such a rich tradition of stories about fire-breathing, winged serpents? One answer can be found in the most famous dragon story of all, the tale of Saint George.

George was a real person. Whether or not he actually slew his notorious dragon, we'll never know. But years after his death, he was granted sainthood by the Catholic church, and his legend grew. European crusaders of the 10th, 11th, and 12th centuries used his story as an example of Christian faith overcoming great obstacles. The dragon represented the forces of evil.

Above: Dragon Perched, by Don Maitz.

As crusaders returned home from the Middle East, they brought with them the story of Saint George, and especially the battle against the dragon. George eventually became a patron saint of England. His slaying of the dragon became a very popular symbol in folk literature, showing up frequently in paintings and books. Troubadours of the 14th century sang his story, and the myth of the dragon, the legendary beast that represented the forces of evil and chaos, became firmly cemented in the minds of common people.

Saint George and the Dragon

Above: St. George and the Dragon, by Paolo Uccello.

One day, at the dawn of the fourth century, in the town of Silene, in Libya, a huge, reptilian creature emerged from the nearby swamplands and began terrorizing the countryside. It was a dragon, with bat-like wings, four legs, a spiraling tail, and thick skin covered with armored green scales, like a crocodile's. When it opened its gaping mouth, foul gas spewed forth, poisoning everything it touched. People who breathed in the noxious fumes were dropped instantly, only to be dragged off to the swamps and eaten by the terrible beast.

The king of Silene tried to calm the dragon by feeding it two sheep each day. Soon, however, the town ran out of sheep, and the dragon once more terrorized the city. The king decided, very reluctantly, that the only way to save his people was to sacrifice a child each day, with the hope that this would quench the dragon's appetite. A lottery was created, and every child under 14 became eligible for the sacrifice. The king prayed that a miracle would soon save them from the evil monster.

After weeks of feeding the beast, no miracle appeared. Then, the king's own daughter, Aleyone, was chosen by the lottery. In the morning, she was tied to a stake at the edge of the swamp. The king could only watch helplessly in despair.

As the princess stood awaiting her fate, she suddenly felt the ground shaking underfoot. But instead of the dragon, a knight in silver armor, with a crimson cross painted on his breastplate, came galloping up on a great white charger. He was armed with a long, wicked-looking lance and white shield. The knight dismounted and identified himself. His name, he said, was George. He was from eastern Turkey, and had been a cavalryman in the Roman army before converting to Christianity. Now he roamed the countryside, assisting those in need.

The princess begged George to flee while he still had the chance. Instead, George untied her. He turned toward the swamp; something large was rustling in the reeds. Then the dragon burst forth, dripping slime and roaring in anger. Its brightly colored scales glinted in the sunlight, and its corkscrew tail thrashed from side to side. Glistening fangs gnashed in a huge, gaping jaw that stank of raw meat. The beast, spotting George, roared with fury.

George raised his lance to strike. Suddenly, the dragon spread

Above: Death of the Last Dragon, by Don Maitz.

its leathery wings. George took a step back in amazement. He seemed to be confronted by hundreds of evil eyes staring back at him. The eye-like spots, which were visible on the underside of the wings, shimmered and shook as the dragon roared, nearly hypnotizing the knight. George shook his head, remembering his vow to help the weak. With all his strength, he thrust his lance forward. The dragon roared and screeched, mortally wounded in the neck.

George and Aleyone led the bleeding dragon back to Silene, where George then beheaded the beast in front of the townspeople, demonstrating the power of his faith against the forces of evil.

SERPENT DRAGONS

People who study dragons are called "dracontologists." Many of these scholars believe that sightings of large snakes led to the myths of dragons. This makes sense when you consider that many of the earliest dragon sightings were of large, serpent-like creatures.

Serpent dragons, called guivres, are the earliest, most primitive form of dragons. Like snakes, they have no limbs, and are wingless. Also called worms (or wyrms) these dragons have horned heads and powerful jaws, like a crocodile's. Worms make their homes near bodies of water, such as lakes and streams, sometimes even the ocean.

Many worm stories come from England, France, and Scandinavia. But their true range is worldwide. Some Native American tribes tell the legend of weewilmekq, a horned serpent that resembles a giant leech!

Facing page: The Biblical sea serpent Leviathan.
Below: An oarfish.

The Bible tells of a serpent dragon named Leviathan, a gigantic monster that lived in the sea. It was so immense that when it thrashed through the water, the sea boiled behind the great beast. Steam hissed from its nostrils, and clouds of smoke and flame spewed from its gigantic jaws. Norse mythology tells of a similar serpent, Jormungander, whose immense coils circle the entire earth.

Some legends of serpent dragons in the sea may have come from sightings of the oarfish. These rare, deep-sea creatures are long and slender, bright yellow in color, with a raised dorsal fin on the back of its head. They can reach lengths of up to 60 feet (18 m).

Above: A gargoyle sits atop Notre-Dame Cathedral in Paris, France.

One serpent dragon that was definitely not an oarfish was the gargoyle of Rouen, France. This medieval town, in the year 520, was terrorized by a serpent dragon that lived in the River Seine. When it first appeared, the tale says, it opened its mouth and great jets of water spewed out, flooding the countryside. Many people were either eaten by the dragon or drowned by the tidal waves. The townspeople called the creature the gargouille, which in the French language means "gargler." Many medieval buildings, such as the cathedral of Notre Dame in Paris, can be seen today with water spouts shaped like gargoyles, designed to drain away rainwater.

The Tale of the Lambton Worm

During the Middle Ages, a curse terrorized the small village of Washington, which lay near the River Wear in County Durham, England. The year was 1420. A boy by the name of John Lambton, the heir to nearby Lambton Castle, decided to go fishing. It was a Sunday, and he had been warned that it was unlucky to skip church, but he was determined to wet his line and fritter the day away.

Young John sat on the banks of River Wear and cast his line. But he caught no fish that day. Instead, his only catch was an ugly worm, which dripped slime and had the face of a demon. In anger, John threw the worm down a well.

Years passed. John grew into a young man, and soon found himself fighting a war in a distant land. Meanwhile, back in the village, something terrible crawled out of the well. The worm John had cast down had grown, year after year, into a huge serpent dragon. Now it lurched across the land, killing cows and chickens, and even young children. It was so gigantic that it could wrap itself around a nearby hill nine times!

When John returned from the war, he was shocked to see his kingdom under siege by the foul beast. He sought a friendly witch's advice on how to slay the evil dragon. She told him he could kill the dragon, but only if he wore a special suit of armor with sharp blades built all around it. She also said that, after killing the beast, he would have to kill the very next living thing he saw, or else a terrible curse would fall on his family.

John quickly had the suit of armor constructed, then set out to do battle with the Lambton Worm. It was a fierce fight. The dragon's powerful jaws opened and snapped as the beast tried to bite the young prince in two. But John was quick on his feet, and skillful with a sword.

Suddenly, John slipped and stumbled into the river, his guard dropping for just a moment. Seeing its chance, the dragon wrapped its immense coils around the brave knight and tried to crush him to death. But the tighter the dragon squeezed, the more the blades encrusted in the armor sliced into its hide. The dragon howled in pain and surprise. John hacked away at the dragon until, finally, it fell in small pieces into the river, and was carried away by the current. John had saved his kingdom from the awful dragon.

John's father, the king, was overjoyed that his son had survived, and came bounding out of the castle to greet him. John realized that his father was the first living thing that he had seen since killing the dragon. But he could not do as the old witch had told him. Instead, he killed his most faithful dog, in hopes that this sacrifice would be enough. It was not. For the next nine generations, a curse fell upon the Lambton family. Every heir to the throne met a tragic end, doomed to die far from home.

Above: John Lambton accidentally hooks a serpent dragon.

CLASSICAL DRAGONS

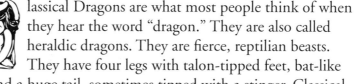

lassical Dragons are what most people think of when they hear the word "dragon." They are also called heraldic dragons. They are fierce, reptilian beasts. They have four legs with talon-tipped feet, bat-like wings, and a huge tail, sometimes tipped with a stinger. Classical dragons usually breathe fire or poisonous gas. They have thick, multi-hued scales, and a head like a crocodile, with horns and razor-sharp fangs.

Far right: A wizard rides a classical dragon in Don Maitz's *Booked Flight.*
Below: Dragon's Run, by fantasy illustrator Janny Wurts.

When Saint George fought his famous duel in Libya, it was with a classical dragon. Another famous encounter with this kind of dragon is told in the ancient saga of Beowulf.

Beowulf is a very old epic poem, written in Old English in approximately 1000 A.D. It tells the story of a mighty sixth century Scandinavian warrior. The story begins in Beowulf's youth, when he saved a Danish city from the monster Grendel, and Grendel's water-troll mother. Beowulf was skilled in battle, and a wise leader. He soon became king of the Geats, a tribe in southern Sweden.

Beowulf Versus the Dragon

When Beowulf became an older man, his land was threatened by a fire dragon. The dragon had become enraged when one of its trinkets, a piece of its treasure hoard which it jealously guarded in an underground lair, was stolen by a peasant. Now the dragon wreaked vengeance upon the humans living nearby.

Beowulf rushed to the cave of the dragon. He called to it, demanding that it come out and fight. Together with a faithful servant, Beowulf battled the hideous beast. The dragon belched flames at the hero-king, but Beowulf was protected from behind his mighty shield.

Beowulf rushed at the dragon and struck, but his sword broke against the creature's scales. As he reached for his dagger, the dragon bit him in the neck and tossed him about like a rag doll.

Suddenly, Beowulf's servant thrust his sword into the soft underbelly of the beast. The dragon released Beowulf and howled. The warrior and his servant hacked at the dragon until, finally, it lay dead at their feet.

Beowulf was triumphant over the dragon, but its bite was deadly poisonous. The mighty warrior died on the spot, victim of the serpent he had just slain.

Right: Darkness at Sethanon, by Don Maitz.

SEMI-DRAGONS

Semi-dragons are a kind of cross between classical dragons and serpent dragons. There are two main types of semi-dragons: lindorms and wyverns. Lindorms have two legs and no wings. They are very serpent-like. Wyverns, on the other hand, have a pair of legs, but a set of wings as well, which makes them appear more like classical dragons.

The most famous lindorm can be found in the tale of Siegfried and the slaying of Fafnir. Siegfried was a hero from ancient German and Norse literature. In one of his adventures, he set out into the countryside to retake the treasure guarded by an enchanted dragon named Fafnir.

Fafnir was a terrible, fire-breathing lindorm dragon who stood watch over a vast hoard of treasure in a deep, dark cave. His scaly armor was nearly impregnable.

Far right: Siegfried slays the lindorm dragon Fafnir. *Below:* A man does battle with a wyvern.

When Siegfried arrived, the dragon was gone on his daily drink at a nearby stream. Siegfried dug a pit in the path where the dragon moved, jumped in, and then waited with his magical sword Gram.

Soon, Fafnir came lumbering up the path. Patiently, Siegfried waited until the dragon moved over the pit, exposing his soft, unprotected belly. Siegfried thrust his sword up, mortally wounding the dragon. Fafnir roared, then collapsed dead, giving up his treasure hoard to the victorious Siegfried.

ASIAN DRAGONS

Dragons appear all over Asia, including Japan and Korea, but especially in China, where they are thought to bring prosperity and good fortune. In China, the dragon is the supreme being of all creatures on earth and in the heavens.

Chinese dragons are quite different from their cousins in the West. They fly, but with the use of magic, not wings. Instead of being angry and jealous, these dragons are energetic and intelligent. They symbolize power and heroism. Dragons of the East can be friendly and wise. They are not hated beasts. Instead, people love and worship them, especially since dragons control the rains and the seas. Farmers often pray to "lung," as dragons are called in China, asking for rain to water their crops.

Below: A painting of dragons from Korea.

Most Asian dragons live in the water. Almost every lake, river, or pond has a dragon spirit that dwells under the surface. Even today, dragon shrines and altars can be seen along seashores and riverbanks of modern China and Japan.

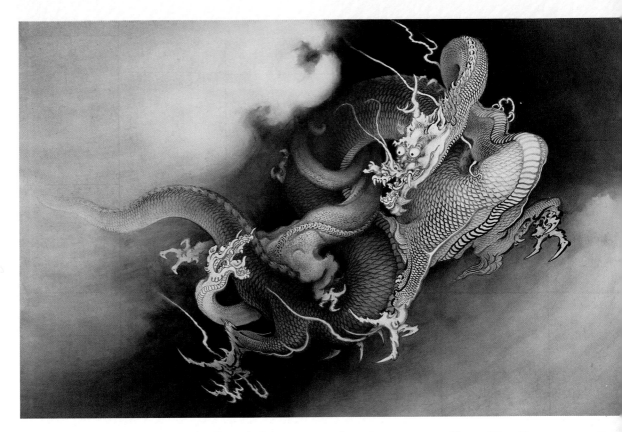

Symbols of dragons can be found almost everywhere in China. Dragon festivals occur regularly, including races in large boats shaped like dragons. During the Chinese New Year, which usually takes place between the end of January and mid February, people dress in immense paper dragons and parade through the streets. Every 12 years of the Chinese calendar is called the Year of the Dragon, which is considered a lucky year.

Since ancient times, the emperor of China claimed to be descended from dragons. Many other Asian rulers also claim to have dragon ancestors. Dragons became a symbol of imperial power. In China, the emperor sat on the "dragon throne." Calling an Asian ruler "dragon face" meant that you were paying him a great compliment. Imperial dragons were shown with five claws, instead of the usual four. Anyone besides the emperor caught with a five-clawed dragon, either in print or sculpture, was subject to severe penalty, even death.

Wise, heavenly, able to ward off evil spirits, and protectors of the innocent, Asian dragons are a symbol of Mother Nature and bringers of life and good fortune.

Above: Two Dragons in Clouds, by Kano Hogai.

DRAGONS TODAY

Since ancient times, dragons have captured people's imagination, and this continues today in books and movies. From *Shrek* to Harry Potter, dragons continue to delight and terrify us.

One of the most popular novels printed in 2003 is *Eragon*, by Christopher Paolini, who was just 15 when he started writing the book. It tells the story of Eragon, a young farm boy, who finds a marvelous blue egg that hatches into a dragon. Eragon raises the dragon, and together they set out on a journey of magic and power.

The villain in J.R.R. Tolkien's *The Hobbit* is Smaug, a red dragon who guards the Dwarven riches deep within Lonely Mountain. Tolkien wrote this fantastical book before moving on to his epic trilogy, *The Lord of the Rings*. Tolkien's character descriptions are a sheer delight: "There he lay, a vast red-golden dragon, fast asleep; a thrumming came from his jaws and nostrils, and wisps of smoke, but his fires were low in slumber. Beneath him under all his limbs and his huge coiled tail, and about him on all sides stretching away across the unseen floors, lay countless piles of precious things, gold wrought and unwrought, gems and jewels, and silver red-stained in the ruddy light."—J.R.R. Tolkein, *The Hobbit*.

In film and video, too, we encounter dragons in an endless variety, from *Dragonheart* to *Sleeping Beauty*, and from *Mulan* to *Reign of Fire*. Dragons seem to be a never-ending source of inspiration for filmmakers.

Dragon stories have existed for thousands of years, all designed to frighten, educate, amuse, and entertain us. Dragons, the very symbol of mystery and power, will be with us always.

Far right: Dragon's Pawn, by fantasy author and artist Janny Wurts.

GLOSSARY

CHARGER

A horse that is ridden into battle, or in a parade.

CRUSADES

A series of military campaigns that took place from the 11th through the 13th centuries. The Crusades began as an effort by western European Christians to recapture Muslim-controlled Jerusalem. They developed into territorial wars, and included much of the Middle East, as well as other "pagan" areas such as the Baltic region of northern Europe.

FOLKLORE

The unwritten traditions, legends, and customs of a culture. Folklore is usually passed down by word of mouth from generation to generation.

GENRE

A type, or kind, of a work of art. In literature, a genre is distinguished by a common subject, theme or style. Some genres include fantasy, science fiction, and mystery.

IMPENETRABLE

An object or barrier that cannot be penetrated, or passed through.

IMPREGNABLE

A place that is seemingly impossible to capture or enter by force. Some medieval castles were built so strong that they were considered to be impregnable by enemy armies.

LAIR
The resting place of a wild animal, usually hidden. Dragons often have lairs deep in caves, where they guard their treasure.

LANCE
A thrusting weapon often used by medieval warriors. Lances usually consist of a long wooden shaft tipped with a sharp metal spearhead. In medieval Europe, knights armed with lances sometimes fought each other on horseback, either in battle or in tournaments.

Marco Polo
Marco Polo was a 13th-century merchant and explorer from the present-day city of Venice, Italy. He was one of the first Europeans to reach China overland.

MEDIEVAL
Something from the Middle Ages.

Middle Ages
In European history, a period defined by historians as between 476 A.D. and 1450 A.D.

MYTHOLOGY
The study or collection of myths. Myths are traditional stories collected by a culture. Their authors are almost always unknown. Myths explain the origin of mankind, or of civilizations. They also explain the customs or religions of a people. Myths are often stories that include the deeds of gods and great heroes.

Norse
The people, language, or culture of Scandinavia, especially medieval Scandinavia.

SERPENT
A serpent is a snake, especially a large or poisonous one.

SLAY
To kill or destroy violently.

TROUBADOUR
Poet-musicians of the 11th through 13th centuries. Troubadours wandered the countrysides of France, Spain, and Italy, telling poems and singing songs of love and chivalry.

INDEX